Canoe Country

ALSO PUBLISHED BY
THE UNIVERSITY OF MINNESOTA PRESS

Snowshoe Country
Florence Page Jaques
Illustrations by Francis Lee Jaques

The Geese Fly High
Florence Page Jaques
Illustrations by Francis Lee Jaques

Canoe Country

by
FLORENCE PAGE JAQUES

illustrations by
FRANCIS LEE JAQUES

University of Minnesota Press | Minneapolis | London

THE FESLER–LAMPERT MINNESOTA HERITAGE BOOK SERIES
This series reprints significant books that enhance our understanding and appreciation of Minnesota and the Upper Midwest. It is supported by the generous assistance of the John K. and Elsie Lampert Fesler Fund and by the interest and contribution of the late Elizabeth P. Fesler and David R. Fesler.

Canoe Country was first published in hardcover by the University of Minnesota Press in 1938. Our knowledge and appreciation of the culture and history of this region have advanced considerably since the book was first published, and some of the attitudes and opinions expressed in its text are not appropriate and the language is at times offensive. *Canoe Country* is reprinted here in its original form to present the book accurately within Minnesota's literary heritage.

Published by the University of Minnesota Press
111 Third Avenue South, Suite 290
Minneapolis, MN 55401-2520
http://www.upress.umn.edu

ISBN 978-1-5179-1272-7 (pb)
A Cataloging-in-Publication record for this book is available from the Library of Congress.

Printed in the United States of America on acid-free paper

The University of Minnesota is an equal-opportunity educator and employer.

30 29 28 27 26 25 24 23 22 21   10 9 8 7 6 5 4 3 2 1

LIST OF ILLUSTRATIONS

Canoe Country

"I'll always turn to the North!" said Lee.

He had been talking about the jungle trails on Barro Colorado Island, in Panama. Till my mind was a whirl of howling monkeys and motmots swinging, scarlet passion flowers and peccaries and blazing blue butterflies.

"Why don't we go to the tropics on our next vacation?"

"I'd rather show you the North," Lee insisted. "Alaska, the Aleutian Islands, Hudson Bay —"

"But the Arctic is either cold or swampy. I know I'd revel in constant balminess, and the bursts of tropic color — whole trees of golden blossoms, and faint rose —"

"Listen. I grant you the tropics are beautiful. But the design is too intricate. Now, in the North you may have one line for the tundra, one for a maroon hill, and another for the snow mountains. Only three lines in the whole landscape. But *what* lines they are! I tell you, the Arctic has character, and composition."

"Yes, my lamb, I know you like the Arctic. But *I* can't revel in starkness. I do want to see solitary places, Lee. But I want to be able to lie down on my back and look at the sky —"

9

"You can't lie down, or even sit down, out of doors in Panama. If you stop one minute, the ticks and red bugs get you."

"Oh —" I was rather baffled. "Anyway, I like trees."

Lee shook his head. "I'll have to take you to the southern limit of the North! What about my state? What about northern Minnesota sometime?"

"That's not arctic."

"It's not so far from it. The muskeg comes down there, and we certainly have winter weather. . . . I wish we could see it this minute; snow means something *there*." Lee looked with intense scorn at the perfectly adequate snow storm outside our windows, whirling around corners and blurring the towers far up the street quite recklessly enough, it seemed to me.

"I wish we were there now," he repeated. "I'd like you to see the pines and tamaracks in three feet of snow. You ought to hear the snow screech under the sled runners, and trees crack in the silence, at twenty below zero."

"I'll go in summer," I said firmly.

"Or early spring, with the horned larks on the fence posts along the snowy roads. Or October. We could hunt prairie chickens then, through the fields."

I began to think of all the things Lee had told me of his Minnesota home. The great stretches of woods where he had hunted deer in his boyhood. The immense skies. Seven Oaks, the house of hand-hewn logs, built by some pioneer and discovered by Lee's mother and father when they came to that country; a house set, with its oaks around it, in a deep curve of the Mississippi. The Mississippi itself, only a small river in that northern land, where Lee used to watch logs floating down to the mills, and the stern-wheeled steamers traveling in summer. The old state road, where the four-horse teams hauled provisions to the lumber camps all through the winter. . . .

10

"I do want to see Minnesota before it loses every trace of pioneer life. But I'll go in summer," I reiterated.

"Of course, if we went in summer I could take you into the Arrowhead country," Lee admitted.

"Yes! What about that canoe country? After all your tales and promises, Othello! Have you ever taken me?"

"Well, why not go? This summer?"

We looked at each other questioningly. Then hopefully.

Perhaps we really shall.

Sunday, February 27th

It has been raining furiously all day long. I'm glad it has.

This afternoon we unearthed the canoe country maps. Lee has shown them to me before and I've always looked at them with sedate interest — never with the catches of breath they gave me today.

There's one huge map of the lake country in general, all the way from the international boundary to the Arctic and from Lake Superior to the Lake of the Woods, nearly to Winnipeg. Another is a detailed map of the Arrowhead itself, the Quetico reserve in Canada and the Superior National Forest in Minnesota, the borderland of both countries. Then smaller maps, some of which Lee helped to make.

I can hardly believe in that country. Hundreds and hundreds of lakes scattered through forest, like pieces of a mammoth jigsaw puzzle scattered over a table. Scraps of rivers lace the lakes together. There are no roads, no paths except short portages; one can travel only by water.

We hung over the maps till I could see curled waves and minute pine trees all over them. I found "This Man's Lake" and "That Man's Lake," with a forlorn little "No Man's Lake" tucked in between and an "Other Man's Lake" farther on. We traced out all Lee's former canoe trips, and he showered me with incredible numbers of old snapshots, to illustrate his explanations. They were most beautiful photographs.

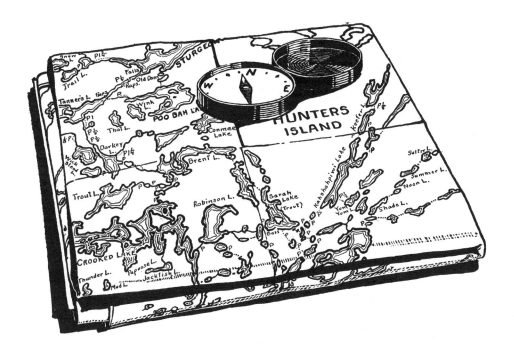

"Lee, we *must* go," I cried.

He disappeared, and came back, to my amazement, with a stepladder. It seemed a peculiar answer to my exclamation. Were we to take off immediately, with the stepladder for airplane? But no. Mounting it, he began to excavate the top recesses of the studio closet.

"What *are* you after?"

". . . see what I've saved from my equipment," he muttered, and began to hand down the canvas bundles and packsacks which have always been mysteries to me.

I don't know how we progressed from studio to living room, but soon we had the latter ornamented with a small tent, an axe, a bevy of pails that fitted into each other with marvelous precision, tin plates, scores of small cloth bags ("you carry all the food in those; you can't pack the extra weight of boxes and cans"), fishing tackle, a coffee pot, a skillet, besides the maps and pictures scattered like leaves after a storm.

Of course it had to be the immaculate Bartons who called at this moment, with two German ornithologists in tow. It couldn't have been any of our intimate acquaintances.

To brush aside Mrs. Barton's magnificent pretense that there was nothing at all extraordinary about our living room *décor*, we had to explain, "We're going on a canoe trip this summer."

So we are committed now. What fun!

Duluth, Minnesota
August 21st

I've never been so cold in my life. I wear my fur coat all the time. If this is what Duluth is like in August what must it be in January!

"Of course," people tell me cheerily, "you'll be much colder camping out."

And I can't take this fur coat with me.

"Three weeks!" they say. "And you've never camped before? Better make it one!"

Three weeks does take careful planning. We must remember everything; there is no place to buy or borrow. And to pack house and furnishings and food inside one small canoe is quite puzzling. Today we've been sorting out our equipment in Aunt Mary's garden, while the next-door children ran around and over us like beetles in wild excitement.

Lee's canoe is intact and is ready to ship to Winton. Our tent is so small it's laughable. Seven by seven, with a ground cloth to match, it ties up in front by one rope to a pole or tree. We're taking an air mattress, an air pillow, and a blanket roll.

There are three packsacks, one for food, another for clothes (with a waterproof bag that holds our toilet articles and a small medicine case), and a third for miscellaneous articles—fishing tackle, films, Lee's sketching outfit, my notebooks, canoe glue, an axe, flashlights, etc. We aren't allowed to take a gun.

We have gone over our list of provisions again and again. The food must be nourishing and yet as concentrated in bulk as it can possibly be. Each purchase is now neatly tied into its little cloth bag. Except the butter — it goes in a can. This is our list:

5 lbs ham	2 lbs salt (we salt the fish to keep it)
5 lbs bacon	
2 lbs dried beef	1 can pepper
1 can corned beef	4 lbs sweet chocolate
1 can veal loaf	2 lbs cheese
3 cans Crisco	2 cans soluble coffee
2 lbs butter	1 can lemon powder (for lemonade)
10 lbs flour	
1 can baking powder	5 lbs brown sugar (for syrup as well as sugar)
4 loaves bread	
1 package rye crisp	1 can powdered milk
2 lbs raisins	2 bars soap
3 lbs apricots	1 cake Sapolio
3 lbs prunes	6 candles
4 lbs dried beans	1 box matches (another in miscellaneous pack)
2 lbs dried peas (a mistake)	

It seems what the women's magazines might call a Meager Menu. Of course if we were taking a guide we could live much more luxuriously, with canned vegetables and even an oven. But a guide would bring civilization into our trip; we would have a buffer between us and the wilderness. As it is, we're facing nature as I, at least, never have before in my life.

As for reading, I'm afraid I'm going to do less of that in the next few weeks than I've ever done in the same length of time. I have three paper-bound reprints, and an old copy of *The King's Henchman*, which hasn't any cover!

I did want to take along some of the vivid stories of explorers and fur

traders, especially the earliest ones, Radisson and Du Luth, for instance, and La Vérendrye (Pierre Gaultier de Varennes de la Vérendrye, to be exact), who with his sons built a string of forts along this route.

Most of all I wanted to take the account Radisson wrote for some of his patrons in England. Radisson was a dashing scamp, perhaps the first white man ever to set foot in this Arrowhead country, and his charm and high spirits (to say nothing of his imagination!) are evident in these *Voyages* of his. Nor can I bear to leave behind the quaint journals of traders like Peter Pond, Macdonell, Hugh Faries, and Nicholas Garry, exact and enthralling accounts of early canoe trips. But books are far too bulky. I must be content with the notebook into which I've copied my favorite passages.

I've warned my family at home that they won't hear from us for three weeks. We'll probably be able to send them some word, Lee says, but since we may not have a chance, it is better for them not to expect letters.

Thursday, August 25th

We have started!

I did appreciate our train's thoughtfulness in leaving Duluth so early yesterday morning; I could not have waited another half-day.

In the early afternoon we disembarked at Winton. Quite unreasonably, I'd been taking it for granted that we would start out from a long pier by a summer inn, with gay launches about and bright flags flying, people promenading in smart sport clothes, so that I'd feel rather conspicuous and shabby in my corduroys and packsacks, before we escaped from sight.

So I felt relieved, though astonished, when we left the train, to find only a dingy country town. The single unusual sight was an Indian family boarding the train: a fat chief, three women in scarlet and orange, and a small Indian boy with a huge basket of blueberries. One of the women had a papoose strapped to her back, which rather surprised me. I thought that custom had vanished long ago.

Lee saw that our canoe came out of the baggage car safely, and we went up to the general store to collect our last supplies. I changed from my traveling things to my corduroy outfit in the attic storeroom, we left our civilized baggage there, and the storekeeper loaded us, our canoe, and packsacks into a truck, took us out, and dropped us along a country road. It all seemed very casual.

Beyond a russet barn, a lake of gentian blue shimmered bright down a grassy hill. We carried everything down to a sketchy dock, we put our canoe in the water, our packs and ourselves in the canoe, and started off.

It was as simple as that.

At first, as we swung out and dipped our paddles into liquid sapphire, the ghosts of the sawmills which used to be so busy here stood all about us. When we got beyond their ruin, and passed summer cottages and boathouses for an hour or more, it was like being on the water at home. This was a mild beginning for adventure.

But when we came to our first portage path, and I helped to unload the canoe, and took the shadowy way with a pack on my shoulders, I felt this was a new experience after all. I carried the clothes pack, Lee took the miscellaneous sack on his back and lifted the canoe — with the paddles lashed in — over his head, so that the yoke fitted to his shoulders. The second trip he took the food pack and blanket roll, while I carried the camera, field glasses, and other odds and ends. I liked tramping over the portage twice with loads; I liked the smell of hot pines and the curve of ferns, the glimpse of dazzling water ahead.

We went down the second lake. Lee settled the packs lower, to lessen wind resistance as well as to steady the canoe. By sunset we had landed on a scrap of peninsula, I had watched Lee cut down a leafy poplar for our first tent pole, and had cooked my first supper over a campfire. Afterward, as we sat on the rocks in the afterglow, a muskrat swam across the

duskiness — our first wild animal. I waved a benediction at him before I went to bed.

Before I left New York, I had wondered whether it would not seem a little desolate to sleep on the ground in a tent, and if the night noises would keep me awake and restless. Even Nicholas Garry's diary did not entirely reassure me. "Nor Ghosts, nor Rattlesnakes, nor Spiders," he said, comfortingly, "nothing can prevent the fatigued Voyageur from sleeping." I had only hoped that I would be as unperturbed.

But now, as I crept between the blankets, I was far too drowsy to realize I was sleeping out of doors for the first time in my life. I went to sleep without a thought for my surroundings.

But this morning, the white mist about us, the exultant laughter of the loons (Lee's favorite birds in this country), made me feel I was really in a different land.

I've just learned how to break camp. There are two inviolable rules.

First, to leave the camping place as
unscarred as possible. Every bit of litter must
be burned or carefully hidden, so that we haven't made the forest uglier
by our presence.

Second, and even more important, every spark of fire must be completely extinguished. To cause immense destruction or perhaps death, because we hadn't taken the trouble to carry another pail of water, or wait
an extra minute, would be horrible.

We are starting now on our first long day's voyage. It is a blue and
immaculate morning, with a quiet wind pacing along with us.

I insist that I should be initiated, as each new *voyageur* was on enter-
ing this country, by being sprinkled with a cedar bough, with appropriate

ceremony, even if we can't manage "a dozen of gunshots fired one after another in an Indian manner." But Lee says that since I haven't a trapping license I am not really a *voyageur*, only a *coureur de bois*. Or should it be *coureuse?*

The loons are flying above us, still laughing. I would like to laugh as jubilantly, at all the people who said I wouldn't like a canoe trip!

Late afternoon

Now we are in the true forest; no more cabins since we left the forest ranger's, where we got our Canadian fishing license, this noon. We have been following the international boundary marks, which trace the ancient canoe route of the Indians. This morning we landed on a sand beach in the United States, to go swimming in the green and orange water; so we decided we would make camp in Canada this afternoon.

What a way to travel — no trains to catch, no traffic to annoy us, no towns to reach by evening, no appointments to remember! We wander anywhere our whims take us, through these lakes and rivers.

Freedom surrounds us. We are finding more than peace here. This is an authentic and profound release from modern intricacies.

I caught the rhythm of paddling today, so that the paddle, the canoe, and I were all one. The monotony of the dip, the push, and the swing has a peculiar fascination after a while. But my shoulders and back are still remembering it.

Our camp tonight is under an enormous white pine, by rapids of dark green glass and snow. Norway pines darken the rocky hill. The ground is covered with blueberry plants, thick with blue lusters. It seems a crime to eat these berries of lapis lazuli, but when we discovered them we never thought of aesthetic scruples — we seized them with both hands.

I speak with such authority about the white and Norway pines, because I've just been learning, from shining examples on the shore, the differences between them. The white is the one with the beautiful horizontal

masses. Its three-sided needles, blue-green and
pliable, come in clusters of five, and its grayish bark
is rough and deeply grooved in old trees. The Norway is straight and tall
(though it cannot reach the height of the largest white pines) with a
reddish trunk. Its stiff dark green needles, flat on one side and rounded
on the other, come in clusters of two.

I've just been down the rocks picking up decorative pine cones for my
campfire. There was a runaway little kingfisher on a twig, pretending to
be an austere and steady fisherman. But he had his father's best white col-
lar on, much too big for him — it came to his eyes — while his hair stuck
up straight with excitement and his tiny feet clutched the twig so ar-
dently I know he was inwardly overwhelmed by his venture.

Lee is fishing too. He has gone over to a narrow island to fish the rapids. Two packsacks lie inside the tent; the third one, with the food and cooking things, keeps me company here. We'll have pancakes and coffee tonight, fish perhaps, certainly blueberries.

Night

While Lee was across the rapids, he caught a ponderous pickerel, and also caught the fishhook in his hand. It came out docilely enough, thank heaven, but when he reached our shore he was bleeding all over the canoe and the rocks and moss, though he was too proud of his capture to notice it. At home I would probably have shrieked and swooned, but here, as there was no one to dash to my aid, I bandaged him up in such a coolly efficient manner that I stood in awed admiration of myself.

As I was serving supper on the rock, I remembered Garry's description of his table, and scrambled in the pack to get my notebook, so that I could read aloud to Lee:

"Our Dinner Table was a hard Rock, no Table Cloth could be cleaner and the surrounding Plants and beautiful Flowers sweetening the Board. Before us the Waterfall, wild romantic, bold. The River Winnipic here impeded by Mountainous Rocks appears to have found a Passage through the Rocks and these, as if still disputing the Power of Water, show their Heads, adding to the rude Wildness of the Scene, producing Whirlpools, Foam loud Noise, and chrystal Whiteness beautifully contrasted with the Black Pine."

It's just the same. What a chance this is, to see granite shores which haven't changed at all, in the three hundred years that have transformed Manhattan from a quiet coast to the most amazing city on earth! To step back in time, and see this country, as the first explorers saw it, as the Indians did when they were its conquerors! Here, one hundred years *is* but a day.

Lee liked the "Whirlpools, Foam loud Noise, and chrystal Whiteness" as much as I did, so I went on to read him Radisson's description of the moose — he calls it sometimes an Eland and sometimes an Oriniack.

"Most of the woods and forests are very thick, so that it was in some places as darke as in a cellar, by reason of the boughs of trees. The snow that falls, being very light, hath not the strength to stopp the eland, which is a mighty strong beast, much like a mule, having a tayle cutt off 2 or 3 or 4 thumbes long, the foot cloven like a stagge. He has a muzzle mighty bigge."

Here Radisson branches off to the "Buff" which "is a furious animal. One must have a care of him . . ." But surely he is talking of the moose again when he says,

"I have seene of their hornes that a man could not lift them from of the ground. They are branchy and flatt in the midle, of which the wild-man makes dishes that can well hold 3 quarts. These hornes fall off every yeare, and it's a thing impossible that they will grow againe."

How can I wait to see an Oriniack!

Friday

We had a sunny and strenuous day's canoeing, with many portages. One very long one, in the late morning, to avoid a series of rapids. The path was so constantly sunny, through small bushes, asters, and goldenrod, up and down hot little hills with rocks to stumble over, that two trips seemed unbearable. I tried to call up visions of La Vérendrye and his sons stalking along this path, of Radisson, debonair and blithe. But I could only picture them in snow or rain or gloom of night. I don't believe they could cope with heat either.

Lunch was on a small hot island under some very unsatisfactory jack pines. These are scrub pines and take all sorts of shapes; we've even seen several solitary ones trying to look like apple trees. How we would have appreciated one like that! But these were contrary creatures, too thin for shade. I felt like shaking shadows out of them.

By keeping our luncheon provisions (just picnic things, cheese crackers, chocolate, and raisins) in the top of the food pack, we don't need to unpack every noon. Simpler and simpler. So after lunching lightly

24

and making lemonade with our lemon powder, we allowed ourselves a short nap. Then on through the hot afternoon.

The rivers were like Peter Pond's favorites, "Verey Gental but Verey Sarpentine." And the lakes were motionless. But we weren't; we were hot and dripping. Who was it told me I'd freeze in this canoe country?

Then Lee decided to teach me to paddle and steer at the same time, and I was not a success. My exertions and Lee's hootings were becoming quite unbearable when, just after three, we turned north away from the international route, and found paradise.

In the first place, we came to a cliff and felt real shade for the first time since early morning. Here we drifted awhile, dipping our hands in the water, and cooling our vivid faces. Then we went on into three small circle lakes which lay, one after another, like strung sapphires.

The island we have chosen to camp on is in the second lake. The first is only half enchanted, but this is wholly so; and as for the third one, it is so bewitched you can't even talk there. I know; we've tried it.

Our own lake is decorated with big round green lily pads and small oval ones of rose and gold. The pine trees stand sedately around it, trailing their reflections in the rippled water, and a flock of little flapper ducks, too young to fly, had it for their own until we came.

Down a very zigzag path—for I was still steering—we came to our chosen island, and its long shadows looked very welcome after the sun's bright glare and Lee's admonitory one. Our tent is on the northern tip of the island. We look out past a great sweep of pine bough to the waters of our lake and the silent misty one beyond.

This is the moment, I think, when I've really given my heart to our canoe country, though I've been entranced with it from the first. But here its special quality of wild innocence touches me sharply and deeply.

I should very much like to live here forever. It's sorcery. It's not our world at all; it's another star.

This evening we set out to acquaint ourselves with our territories. Back to the first lake of the chain, where there were beaver houses to investigate. Then across our own lake again, laughing and talking nonsense.

But at the inlet to the third, we fell silent. If we didn't make a noise, Lee muttered, pretending he could talk if he wanted to, we might see a deer.

The water was without a ripple. Its candid ring was edged with tall bulrushes, spare dark whips exactly reflected. Great pines stood up around it in lovely broken lines, and down a narrow marsh we saw a great blue heron motionless in the tufted grass.

We slipped without a sound through the tranquillity. The rushes slanted above our heads as we floated by.

We came to the channel of an ethereal river, vanishing among the reeds. There was no breath of sound. Great white boulders gleamed here and there in the clear waterway. The rushes massed around us. Along silent curves we slid, on and on, until at last a small rapids rushed down from the black sanctuary of the forest.

Its foamy course broke the silence; we took a breath, and turned our canoe homeward.

It was dusk now, but a faint clear light still held. As we drifted back through the high reeds, great horizontal ripples came slowly toward us through the crystal water. It gave me the oddest sensation — our canoe seemed to be rising straight up into the twilight air. But that would not have been unnatural, after all, in this strange place.

We heard a great horned owl call, far away. Darkness was coming down the hills. In the pale water before me, an otter curved momentarily, and the silver wake of a beaver flashed, far down the other lake.

At the inlet, we could see our small white tent glimmering in the center of the island, in the center of the lake, in the center of the forest. Here was the center of the world.

Saturday

It's cool this morning. I'm writing this in a tall pine wood. Giant pines range up a long hill, with clean open spaces between the bronze trunks instead of all the undergrowth and ferns and twisted branches we usually have. Morning sunlight falls down to the matted needles in bars of brown sunniness and gold mist. The wind tastes fresh, pungent, and wild.

How utterly different this forest land is from the other two I've loved! Fontainebleau, a medieval dream forest (of course we saw it in April); the New Forest, the essence of England's beauty, where Robin Hood might appear down any glade. This country never knew a medieval time; it came straight from the primeval into today. And as for Robin Hood, I can't quite picture him scrambling over logs or hunting moose in a canoe.

We've been up the river. We portaged past the rapids — it seems so easy to portage when the baggage is home in camp! — and on up the stream. We found grassy banks, with spruce behind them, and then burned-over hills, bare and haunted. Giant trunks lay along the banks, their roots and branches distorted in the air. The river became so persistent in its stones and boulders that we could barely push through.

We met our first pileated woodpecker here, high on a charred pine. (At least, *he* was on the charred pine.) He is very shy and is found in the wildest places, so I was glad to have a chance to gaze at him.

He was a stunning bird, about twice as large as our red-headed woodpecker; black with a pattern of white on wings and neck, and a flashing red crest. He looked so powerful I longed to see him attack a tree, for he cuts and chisels like mad, hanging on by his feet and using his whole body for a hammer. Chips and strips of bark fly in every direction, and he sometimes rips off pieces a foot long.

30

But he didn't perform for me. He went away instead, flashing the great spots of white beneath his wings as he flew, and left me lost in admiration.

Lee says the courtship dance of the pileated woodpecker is most extraordinary. The male and female meet on a treetop, spread their pinions wide (they're between two and three feet across) and hop and balance and bow to each other. Sometimes they kiss or feed each other, and then begin their posturing again. What a strange spectacle it would be, against the sky! Often they fly up and wheel in circles through the air, with fluttering wings and pointed crests, and then come down to dance again on the branches. I wish I could see them. I wonder if they look as joyful as the black and white lapwings we saw tumbling down the sky in England.

Saturday Evening

This afternoon we went down to the Painted Rocks and climbed the cliff, to a lake that was lying obstinately on top of the hill, instead of at the bottom where it belonged! We found a very jungle-y place where something had been wallowing. And on the cliff edge were the most enormous blueberries in the world. Hothouse blueberries, almost as big as grapes.

Then, in the canoe, we floated under the Painted Rocks.

On the overhanging cliffs, Lee pointed out to me the vague outlines of moose, in red pigment. The first explorers saw these too. In Macdonell's journal he tells of some at Derraud's Rapids between Lake Huron and the Ottawa River:

"The figure of a man standing over an animal that lays under him, with a sun on one side and a moon on the other . . . A little farthur on is at least 16 figures of different animals standing promiscuously together on the face of a steep Rock . . . painted with some kind of Red Paint."

Above the drawings was a crack into which the Indians used to shoot their arrows. A friend of Lee's once climbed up and found arrowheads there.

It's threatening rain tonight, and Lee is making the tent snug, seeing that the wall canvas is tucked under the floor cloth on every side, and digging a shallow trench around us.

Sunday, August 28th

It did rain last night. It is raining today.

I woke in the night to the sound of rain pounding its tiny fists against the canvas so near our heads. I couldn't believe I was out in such a fragile shelter in the middle of a storm. Such frail walls to hold off such a bombardment. But our tent seemed to be intact and dry, so serenely I folded my hands and went to sleep again.

When I awoke this morning the lake was silver gray, and gray mist dimmed the forests. Our merganser ducks, feeling important, were steamboating like mad around the lake. Twenty-four of them in a proud little line, making reckless splatters in the rain.

We made a pygmy fire of pine cones and twigs, sheltering it between two stones in the tent opening. Just enough of a campfire for hot coffee. With it we ate ham and rye crisp and apricots, and watched from our refuge for ducks or deer. Only some Indians came past in a heavily laden canoe, bound, I suppose, for a reservation up on Lac la Croix.

I had to struggle against an idiotic pity for our canoe, lying on the shore, upside down and shining wet, in the plunging rain! I have become

32

very fond of this companion of ours, which carries us along so resolutely. All the more because one is so thwarted in an affection for a canoe —there's nothing to do for it. If I could only give it a loose rein, or feed it hay or gasoline! But it is completely independent. I can only pat it slightly now and then.

Later it rained more gently, so we put on our raincoats and went out to fish. I decided that fishing in the rain is far more glamorous than fishing in the sun, for the lake was gray moire, the mistiness changed from gray to soft Madonna blue, and the distant islands had dimmed to phantoms of faint violet. The rain made a tiny patting sound on the lily leaves and on our hats.

An osprey circled over the lake searching for fish. Then he sat in the top of a pine and looked down meditatively into the water. *Le Penseur.* I don't know what he caught, but I caught four pike, a bass, and a water lily as lovely as an ivory carving.

33

It is now sitting in a tin cup under the dripping pine, looking as out of place as a duchess in a wheelbarrow.

We arose at the hour of five this morning, to chase a moose we had heard in the night.

Never hear a cow moose in the night, when you don't know what it is! It is the most blood-freezing sound, a wild and wailing whoop, uncanny as Dracula. I heard it first at midnight. "Lee! What is that?"

"Well," he said thoughtfully, "it doesn't sound exactly like wolves!"

If *he* doesn't know what it is, I thought, after all his canoe trips!

"Lee," I said, after thinking wistfully of guns and revolvers, "Lee, where is the axe?"

"Down on the shore by the canoe."

And then that awful howl, much nearer this time. But there wasn't anything to be done and I went back to sleep. However, Lee, hearing it again before daylight, decided it was a lovelorn moose. So he woke me up and we started out to find it.

We couldn't see a thing beyond the rocks where the canoe lay. It was fantastic, launching the canoe into an immensity of fog; we were paddling in a white cloud. But to my relief we didn't fall through.

After a time we got the vaguest of shore lines; by then the lake was so thick with rushes that we slid along through them as if we were paddling in a grassy meadow. We found the mouth of the phantom river and went along, surprising a flock of black ducks and two great blue heron. There were no moose.

On our way back, a deer stirred in the grass along the shore. Lee paddled very gently toward her, while I found I couldn't manage my breath, to say nothing of the field glasses. As we drew near, Lee took only a stroke now and then when she lowered her head to eat, till at last we were in the reeds beside her. When we glided up close to the delicate

34

creature she gazed astonished. Then she whirled off among the upspringing birches.

I had wondered, I'll admit, if a three weeks' trip might not seem monotonous part of the time, in such a complete solitude. But I was wrong. Our life is as full here, for the time being, as it is in New York, with all its companions from every part of the world, its great art and music, its floodtides of ideas.

For every second, every inch, of this experience is filled with utter harmony. We take our way wherever we like; the animals and birds are as good company as one could ask; and if we tried we couldn't find an unsightly spot or a jarring note.

No despairs are here. And no man-made dangers. The bright eyes of the beasts need only look for their natural enemies, and we ourselves can forget all the world's turmoils and antagonisms. This absolute freedom gives every hour an intense lucidity.

Tuesday

We broke camp yesterday morning, breaking our hearts as well, as we left our circle lakes behind us. I couldn't have left if it had been as ethereal as usual, but it was a dull and forbidding morning, with clouds of iron ranging low. After we were well away, however, the day forgot its sullenness.

All day long we came west through the intricacies of Crooked Lake. Lovely river ways, wide stretches of cornflower water, studded islands; shores ranging from great bare hills just touched with delicate green by the young birches and poplars to massive tangled forest.

This was a day with people in it. First, in the morning, we met two boys from St. Paul, going out. They offered to take our mail, so the two canoes clung together for a while, in mid-lake, while Lee talked to the boys about their experiences and I scribbled an enthusiastic letter to the family.

Then at noon, as we passed a low island with a camp on it, we saw a lone man dancing and leaping and shouting wildly. He wasn't in pain, nor were his shouts ecstasy; they were just yells.

In the twilight this would have been quite eerie; even at noon it was grotesque enough — that tousled figure, leaping in the sun.

We didn't know whether he was drunk, or touched by the silence of this country. We had a Chicago friend, a man who had always lived in cities, who came here for an outing but went out the second day. He said he couldn't stand the feeling that there wasn't anyone beyond a hill. Sometimes, they say, when a ranger is here alone for months, he goes slightly mad from the solitary unconfinement.

So, as the dancer didn't call to us for help, I was glad to hurry past this island.

We ate our lunch farther along, with me keeping a wary eye out for a delirious canoe. Much to Lee's amusement, the wretch.

The afternoon freshened, with a gusty wind and high-piled clouds. At first we had many islands, but later in the afternoon we came to the western end of the lake, which was almost a "traverse," as the *voyageurs* called a wide stretch of water. The waves grew choppy enough to make it quite exciting. We lurched and shipped water until I had to bail, for the first time in our journey. I was glad Lee had had so much experience in canoeing.

Lee remembered a very beautiful point near the Curtain Falls, but as we approached it we could see two white tents in among its pines. Baffled — why were *people* around here, anyway? — we went past almost to the falls and found a camp site on a small stony bay, with drooping jack pines on it and a heavy forest behind.

Here we are two Gullivers in Lilliput. We have a great stir of wild life around us, in an extremely small way. Chipmunks by the score gallop around, mad with curiosity. Chickadees swarm in the pines, right side up or upside down, it doesn't seem to matter; their *dee-dee-dee*'s are con-

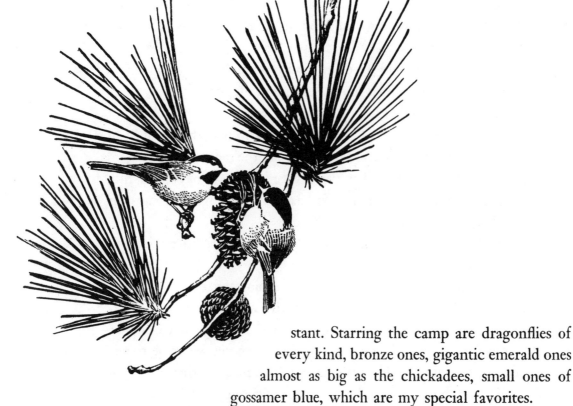

stant. Starring the camp are dragonflies of every kind, bronze ones, gigantic emerald ones almost as big as the chickadees, small ones of gossamer blue, which are my special favorites.

And when I went down the shore to get driftwood, I ran into a migration of yellow warblers, hundreds of them, flicking in and out of the foliage like yellow sparks.

I sat down on a ledge to watch them. My hand against the harsh surface made me think of the stones themselves.

The rock formation of this whole country, I read somewhere, is part of the great Canadian Shield, so called because its surface of more than a million square miles, surrounding Hudson Bay on three sides and coming down into the United States at this point, is in the shape of a vast shield. This shield is of pre-Cambrian rocks, the oldest on the crust of the earth. From 48,000,000 to 1,710,000,000 years old! Those figures made a deep impression.

40

I looked back to those primordial ages, with the sundered stone around me — the stone that is the most ancient thing that we can see or touch in our world. The vastness of this shield and its antiquity was overwhelming me, when the *chee*-ing of the warblers made me turn back to them. Their evanescent yellow feathers flitted as gaily as ever through the cobweb green. I picked up my firewood and went home.

We had our supper on the rocks by the water, with impulsive chipmunks crowding us. One especially, dashing in and out of woodpecker holes like a miniature clown, distracted me terribly from my cooking. After supper I began to wash my dishes, but there was an afterglow of such luminous peach-gold that we left the dishes unregarded on the shore. Floating off into the spacious evening, without a ripple in the clear light above or below us, we set out to see Curtain Falls.

The falls, rough and dangerous, hypnotized me. The black smoothness of the water, just before it curved over the falls, was savagely elemental. We stayed till dark watching it, the spray and the green underswing; listening to the loons call.

When we got back to our point, we still had the Lilliputians about. Two tiny wood mice came out to clear away our crumbs. They were comic things, with their big eyes and round fuzzy ears and bits of whiskers. I felt quite guilty, liking them so much, when I shriek at house mice.

But I was in a liking mood. I even enjoyed washing my dishes, with the black night all about and stars in my rinsing water.

We saw the red sun come up this morning, through white mist. Our customary breakfast, blueberries, flapjacks, bacon, and coffee, tasted unusually good out on our rocks, even though the chipmunks chanted crossly at us because there were no prune seeds. After breakfast we went to Roland Lake portage to find a moose swamp Lee remembered. We found the swamp but no moose.

Only more loons. But they repaid us. I had never before been near enough to see how they run along the water's surface before they fly, and their spattering strides across the lake amused me enormously. Nor had I known before that they can vary their specific gravity at will, so that they float either with their spotted black and white bodies showing or with just the sleek black heads and striped necks above water.

We made a game of timing their long dives under water — they are magnificent submarines — and seeing who could guess how long they would stay submerged. One stayed under four minutes and a half — he was our champion. But they have been known to stay as long as eight minutes.

I hadn't realized before that loons are strictly water birds. They can barely hobble on land, though they make such swift runs on the lakes. And their flying seems to be done under water as well as in the air, for they use their wings as well as their feet in their long dives. They are all mixed up about locomotion. I turn giddy thinking of them, soaring in reverse, with fish about them.

Lee says they have many calls. The common laughing call, *hoo-hoo-hoo-hoo*, and the night call we have heard. Then there is a storm call, and what is known as the "silly song," as well as shorter notes.

Coming back, we met the people who are camping on the point. There were two canoes, a couple in one, in the other a guide and a fat man who, believe it if you can, wore a big white life preserver! He was

42

quite complacent about it, but the red-headed guide looked as shamefaced as a small boy does when a doll is forced upon him.

These voyaging days are translucent with joy. When we start out in the morning, the earth has such a before-Eden look that it seems a shame to shake the dew from the blueberries or strike our paddles into the sleeping water. Thrusting on into sun-filled channels; drifting into green-needled embrasures where chickadees are buoyant; landing on a beach to bathe and to read the overnight paw prints — it is all intoxicating.

Now we have left the smooth pine slopes and the great bare hills of stone. We have come to rugged shores, ancient pines, and huge creviced rocks, rich in tone, padded deep with hoary moss and gray-green lichens. When the lakes are calm, they reflect the most glowing colors, dark wines and purples and crimsons, deep blues and greens, that we haven't noticed on the banks.

Only after we have seen the pure colors in the water do we look up and distinguish them in the tree trunks and cliffs, where we have seen only browns and greens because we weren't expecting anything else. An artist once told me that if you really want to see the color of a landscape you should stand on your head. This of course is practically the same thing.

We are camping on a jagged island in Lac la Croix.

Until now I have been very amenable about our camps. I've liked to go along and never know when Lee would say, "Why not camp here?"

But that is changed. Yesterday on the Curtain Falls portage — by the way, have I said how deeply I approve of portages? After miles of sunny waters, to have a chance to use your legs instead of your arms for propulsion, to plunge into a crisp, shadowed path, sundering ferns and bushes, brushing spiced boughs, a turquoise lake behind, unknown water ahead, feet clinking on the stones! In our doubled trips across, I never get quite

44

used to leaving half of all our worldly
goods sitting unprotected on the rocks. Nor can
I ever take for granted the wood fragrance, so different
from the smell of the air on the lakes. I have pine scent inextricably mixed
with portages now; one will always make me remember the other.

As I was saying, on this portage we met a couple who had been fishing
for deep lake trout. The four of us sat down by the black curves and foam
white of the rapids and talked, mostly about trout. However, Mrs. Morse
did mention casually that they had seen no moose this year but that
wolves seemed unusually prevalent, and so they had preferred to camp on
islands.

So now I prefer to camp on islands too.

I can't help it. Lee teases me, and I know it's foolish, that the wolves
can swim if they're really hungry, that they only get ravenous in winter,

and that even in winter it is extremely doubtful that they ever attack man. But still Mrs. Morse's words reverberate in the air. And after all, why *not* camp on islands?

They're much more interesting than mainlands, which run on and on in an aimless sort of way. Each island we meet has an individuality of its own, serene or careless or aloof. We saw an innocently wanton one clad in nothing but two daisy plants.

Our present island was bequeathed to us by the Morses.

It's just beyond Bottle Portage. It may be the one where Macdonell "Killed a cub Bear and slept in sight of the Mai." The mai was a lobstick or maypole, a favorite landmark of the *voyageur*, made by cutting away most of the branches of a tall tree. I like to think what welcome signs they must have been, just as the international boundary markers are hailed by us with joy.

This is an island with an escarpment, rather high and harsh, around three sides. To the west we have a small harbor, a semicircle of flat clean-washed stones. The center has an open space for our tent, the rest is inexorably wooded, and the thick dark moss under the trees is wonderful to walk on barefoot.

How much more sensitive we are to feeling in this primitive environment! In fact, all five senses are much more wide awake. Of course, one would expect seeing and hearing to be more enjoyable here, since there are only pleasant sights and sounds. And taste is proverbially keener out of doors.

But how much more I notice the touch of things! The smooth paddle in my hand, the shock of cold water on my face, the texture of rough sticks and pine cones when I pick up firewood. The slimness of pine needles in my fingers, the springy turf or hard granite when I step.

And the increased keenness in the sense of smell. I wish we had a better word for *smell* — one that didn't suggest a disagreeable sensation! *Scent, fragrance, odor*, they are all too sweet, too flowery. No, *smell* is what I mean, the different way that early morning smells, and twilight. The changes one forest path can give you as you walk along, the scent of wet green leaves, and dried brown ones, of mushrooms, and crushed grass. . . .

Last night it was cold. There was a hint of a new moon in the apple-green sky, and a wind in the pines all night long. Snug in my blankets, I could imagine that the branches above us still held faint echoes of war drums, or the songs of the *voyageurs:*

> *"Quand j'étais chez mon Père,*
> *Petite Janeton,*
> *Il m'envoyait à la fontaine*
> *Pour pêcher du poisson.*
> *La Violette Dandon, oh!*
> *La Violette dandé. . . ."*

But it's time to get breakfast. Lee has gone over to the other side of the island to see whether a certain eagle is golden or only bald, and I've been scribbling, far too long.

Lee will expect flapjacks when he gets back. I'm an expert flapjack-maker by now, for our bread is all gone. Lee is better at the actual flap, however, for when I do it, the flapjack, instead of turning the customary mild summersault, soars so high that it is quite cold by the time it comes down.

I cook fish very well now; my boiled beans with bacon and my outdoor coffee are delicious. The only things I cannot cook are the dried peas. I have boiled some for three days, carrying them hope-fully along with us, setting them on a fire the minute we stop, and still they rattle

stubbornly when the water bubbles. I mean to give them to this chipmunk
who thinks he helps me cook. He is the smallest one I have ever seen, and
the most engaging. And I'm afraid he knows very well that he is, for he
poses outrageously. Now he is sitting on the very tip of a dead cedar
bough, eating a prune seed, and only glancing at me fleetingly over his
minute shoulder. Sublimely preoccupied!

We were marooned yesterday on a sand beach. We went to see some more painted rocks, even more interesting than the first cliff, with moose and men in war canoes and the prints of many hands, all in bright red.

These paintings make the primitive red man seem startlingly alive, much more so than seeing modern Indian culture ever has. Especially these prints of hands. Real hands . . . I had a ghostly feeling.

While Lee was trying to photograph the paintings, the wind had streamed down against us harder and harder. White plumes filled the lake till Lee thought it was hazardous to attempt the passage back to the island.

So we scurried on, around a more or less sheltered shore, and found a short sand beach between two vertical cliffs. It was a mere dune between the lake and a swamp beyond, but we took refuge there.

Climbing up ponderable rocks of gray and green and orange to a small cave garlanded with vines, we ate a lunch of cheese and chocolate, which Lee happened to have, luckily, in his pocket. Below us the waves pounded against the sand.

Now, as we sat in our cave, sheltered from the strong gusts, a whole family of moose birds gathered around us, looking at us with friendly eyes, cocking their black-capped heads inquisitively.

This fluffy gray bird is a jay, the Canada jay, also called the camp robber and Whisky Jack, the last derived from his Indian name, Wis-ka-tjon. He seems to have no fear of man at all, though he chooses to live in the wild woods instead of around settlements. I had been wanting to see a moose bird, having heard so many tales of his brazenness and robberies.

But I decided today that he is misjudged.

Crows are crafty and clever thieves, taking an ironic pride in their knavery. But the moose bird is so wide-eyed and innocent—I can't believe he thinks he is a robber at all; he just borrows things, feeling sure you won't mind, since he is a friend of yours.

These particular birds sat near us companionably. After a little, Lee set out a crumb of cheese and a crumb of chocolate on the rim of the ledge. Both were snatched up at once. Before long the family was diving and dipping past us, catching slivers of chocolate or cheese or silver paper from our fingers, and perching along the vines. We enjoyed this entertaining in a cave!

After our refreshments had vanished, our guests did too, and we climbed down and explored the hill east of the swamp, till a red squirrel, singing a real little melody up in a tree, saw us and began to scold instead. Really, the animals are as stern with us as they were with Alice in Wonderland. We ruefully made our way back to the beach.

I sat down on the sand and thought delightedly of being reprimanded by a squirrel. I began to realize that one of the deepest joys of this vacation, which I had scarcely been conscious of, is the nature of our social

contacts. So clear, so direct — a squirrel's dislike, the wordless friendship with the jays, the comedy offered by two ants with a flag of dried beef, the awe an ancient pine awakes. After the complicated stresses and emotions a metropolitan day engenders, gatherings where intricate attractions and repulsions web the air, confidences given, advices asked for unsolvable problems, faces in the subway with expressions that tear one's heart . . . Of course one wouldn't want to escape the complex demands forever. But for a breathing space — what a release!

While Lee began a color sketch of the cliff, I lay in the half-shade of tall grass, by a twisted ash tree. When I pillowed my head on my arm I could look along the honey-colored pebbles into a medley of wild-rose briars. Swept by the strong south wind, lulled by the assault of the waves against the sand, I remembered drowsily the first time I ever discovered that poetry had the power to give me cold tingles up and down my back. I could hear the golden voice of our tall young English teacher as clearly as I had when I was thirteen:

> "*And answer made the bold Sir Bedivere:*
> *I heard the ripple washing in the reeds,*
> *And the wild water lapping on the crag. . . .*
>
> *I heard the water lapping on the crag,*
> *And the long ripple washing in the reeds.*"

With that murmur in my mind I drifted off to sleep.

When I woke, the wind was more boisterous than ever, and the waves were storming in, so I went wading down the shore. Of course I got drenched, but it didn't matter; I simply went in swimming. It was glorious! The lake glittered darkly blue, the pines were emerald sequins flashing in the wind. Long tangles of water grass wavered in gold-brown streamers about me, and then the brilliant sand shone clear again through the surge. The waves, rough as half-grown puppies, played about me, tossing me over, pushing me back to land.

At sunset the wind lessened, and we came back to our island camp.

By the way, Lac la Croix seems to have a reputation for marooning travelers. I have a note from Hugh Faries' diary:

Friday, August 17, 1804

"Embarked this morning and proceeded down to Lake Lacroix, but it blew such a strong head wind, that we did not go far forward. . . . Strong wind and clear weather. [Just like today.]"

Saturday, August 18

"Early this morning we proceeded to the little portage La croix tho' it blew very hard a head. at 1 oclock the men went down with a demie charge to the Pines. they return'd at Sunset having damaged their canoes."

Sunday, September 4th

We decided to come exploring down the Bear Trap River. It is the most unfrequented place that Lee can think of, near by, and he hopes we may find moose. Deer we have seen often, though I've only mentioned one — I *can't* seem to get everything in — but all these days and not one moose has appeared. Lee is quite desperate.

The forests were more patrician than usual this morning. Narrow gold diagonals fell through the green-towered ramparts, and the air was cool and touched with fragrance. The water rippled clearly, darkly; outside a shadowy cove the sky to the west bloomed with pale clouds of lavender and faint purple and that creamy fire opals have. I needed some ritual to follow, an orison of worship.

Today we saw our first bear! Lee made me jump by laughing suddenly; he saw it slip from the bluff it was climbing. It fell into the water with a splash, surprising itself and Lee enormously. I was only in time to see a dark shape scramble up the bank, and later, by paddling hard, we had a glimpse of its grotesque silhouette against the skyline for a moment. Lee said that bears will not condescend to hurry if they know you are watching them, but they make up for it as soon as they think they're out of sight.

Later in the morning a gale came up again while we were crossing Iron Lake. The water turned a deep violet, the waves were urgent and white capped. We had to struggle violently to make headway; it was fun, but it was a real combat. Cloud shadows and flashes of sun whirled by us, as we dug our paddles furiously into the surging assault.

"I'll quarter against the wind," Lee shouted to me. "If I drive straight into it, the waves are too close together. We hit too hard."

I was completely exhausted by the time we finally rounded a rugged point and came to smooth, washed shores of pale ivory that were banked by sooty jack pines in close thickets. Here we discovered the mouth of Bear Trap River.

This was a hidden river of abrupt turns and many boulders; remote and casual, it may not have been traversed for many years. A weight of sun lay on its low shores; reeds and rushes and yellow pond lilies, black ducks, blue herons, and bluer kingfishers bedecked it lavishly.

We had lost the wind. It was midsummer and midnoon. We made our way slowly up the river, until we came to a portage. Here was simply

54

an immense face of cliff, seemingly unscalable, blocking the river, which disappeared in an offhand manner.

Even if it hadn't been remorselessly hot, I was sleepy from fighting the waves all morning. I assembled a modest lunch, though untying the strings of the bag seemed an impossible task. "Hurray," I said to myself, as I gazed at the cliff, "that's stopped us. I can have a nap."

But Lee, fascinated beyond words by the disappearance of the river, was enthusiastic about climbing over the cliff to see what we'd find.

I loathed the idea! I felt fuzzy in my knees, my face was a scarlet flare, and I knew I could never drag myself over the half-mile portage the map promised.

Before I could summon energy to express my violent disapproval, Lee was scrambling up the sheer rock with the canoe balanced on his head; so rebelliously I scrambled too.

We reached the top breathless, and I was allowed to lead the way along a lost path in dense forest. Outwardly a guide, but inwardly a whole mutiny. I hated this path as vehemently as I had loved all our other portages.

Nobody had come here for a long time, we could tell. But there were moose and bear tracks, and I had to scrabble through low branches and tangled places, where I couldn't see what I was going to meet.

I kept stumbling and stubbing my toes. I don't know why I always stub my toes when I am cross; it's one of the minor mysteries of life.

We crossed the portage at last and met the river again. It went placidly on, with grass bogs on either side—a perfect place for moose, Lee was sure. The sun was too hot for me even to mention what I knew perfectly well: there wouldn't be any moose.

There weren't any moose. Nothing alive appeared on that river, except a very drowsy turtle on a rock.

We toiled on down the river, until we came to a place where beavers had been gnawing down trees with industrious teeth and building a super-

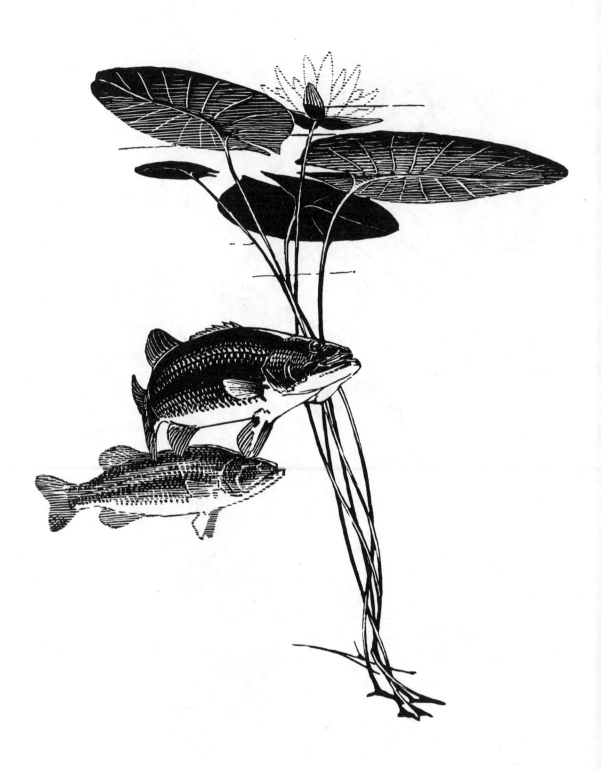

solid dam. Even to contemplate the enormous amount of labor they had lavished on it made me feel shattered. Infuriating, haggard, short-winded beasts beavers must be, I thought, working like that. They'd be proud of themselves, too, for being all worn out. I disliked them heartily. But at least their dam stopped our expedition.

When we had dragged ourselves back to the luggage and embarked again, Lee was not long in finding a place to camp. He indicated a rocky point.

"Splendid to watch for moose here."

But I felt supremely indifferent to moose, and it was a very small point. The next possible place, a jack pine wood, I refused too; it was too closely overgrown. The third discovery was a bare rock slope with a little thicket, and black forest beyond.

"There!" said Lee triumphantly.

"It isn't an island," I murmured.

"Of course it is. See that marsh — it probably leads around to the river again." He looked so hot, poor lamb, that I couldn't insist on more paddling. I accepted the place as a possible island, and we landed here.

Lee made me lie down in the shade of a scraggy pine, while he made camp. I was almost asleep when he came gaily along, to show me that a bear had been overturning rocks in search of ants, just by our tent. Like Queen Victoria, I was *not* amused. What if it comes back for an ant it has overlooked?

This really is a magnificent view, with the river curving widely on one side, and a great grass marsh on the other. But it's aloof and alien to me; this isn't an intimate place. I'm not a part of it as I've been in our other camps. I don't want to stay here longer than one night.

September 5th

Today has been superb! Such sudden changes! And we've had a Noah's Ark of animals all day long.

59

It started badly. When we woke it was still hot and sultry, with a heavy feeling in the air. Forest-fire weather, Lee said, and we had breakfast down by the water, to be especially careful. A dismal breakfast in the sun, with the flapjacks gummy, cold coffee, and no fruit. For I'd forgotten to stew any of the dried fruits and bears have eaten the blueberries from this slope. Also, I spilled the prepared milk. And I felt disgruntled because the management had furnished no sand to scour my skillet, nor any soft thick grass to clear the dishes with.

Never mind. We went off to investigate the eastern swamp, which had an evasive fascination. Rivulets filtered through the slipping grass. Strange plants swayed in the shadowy greenness under our paddles. Little three-petaled flowers, frail as apple blossoms, floated awry in the swamp pools, where tenuous shapes wavered and dissolved. It was a sliding place, without validity.

But a west wind came up, and the air lightened. We found a small stream which led us to a hidden pond. Peering through the ice-green poplars, we discovered six deer bathing in the water! Like nymphs they looked, careless and unafraid. We watched them with delight until a splendid buck suddenly appeared on the far shore. Just for a glancing moment; then he caught our scent, and so we lost them all.

We started back in high spirits, with a kingfisher darting like a blue arrow ahead of us. Then I heard a noise. Like something crying.

"Lee, what is it?"

He listened. "It might be a bear cub."

It was a porcupine, up in a cedar tree, with its head between its paws, crying and crying.

One couldn't comfort a porcupine, but I got out on the bank to see it, and caught sight of another one, climbing a tall poplar. Hand over hand he went, like a man, and then swung hilariously on a high branch in the wind.

As we came back toward camp, Lee saw still another, walking around

60

our tent, the rascal. We were deluged with porcupines. When we reached the tent, we chased the intruder up a tree, and Lee threw my hat at him.

"Why, Lee!" I cried.

However, when I rescued the hat, it was skewered with several of the quills, which come out so easily whenever anything brushes against a

porcupine, and so I could examine the needle point and the myriad barbs along each quill.

The fourth creature appeared down among the lily pads, swimming absurdly with both paws at once. I'd never heard of porcupines in the water, and I didn't expect it of them. Porcupines are so *dry* — it's like seeing a cactus take to swimming. But it seems the quills are slim tubes of air and buoy them up like water wings.

All afternoon was swift with clouds. The wind grew damp with coming rain, while a menace of navy blue piled up in the west.

Lee decided he saw a deer at the end of the bay, and if we slipped down along the grassy bank we would be quite close to her. She was looking so intently across the inlet that she didn't see us until we were within a canoe's length. Then off she went in a tremendous bound.

Then we saw why she had been gazing so steadily. Her spotted fawn had balked on the other bank. It looked at us with great soft eyes. We knew each other intimately, for one moment, before it disappeared.

As we came out into Bear Trap River again, it began to rain. At the same moment, "Moose!" Lee exclaimed.

I caught a glimpse of something brown downstream. Then it disappeared behind an outcrop of rock. What did rain matter when we could realize our ambition at last? We tore downstream. There it was. A cow moose in the water.

62

I stopped paddling; I was too excited not to splash. Then suddenly, beyond her we caught sight of a bull moose!

Two great prehistoric creatures in front of us, like the monsters you see in dreams.

We came closer and closer to them. Till I thought we were quite close enough, and began to talk. Loud enough to be noticed, I hoped.

For moose think very slowly, and they might have been muddle-headed enough to make a wrong turn and plunge into the canoe instead of away from it, if they were very suddenly surprised. Lee is almost too expert at creeping up on creatures.

When they finally did see us, they didn't believe in us. They gazed incredulously as we edged nearer. Then at last they splashed madly through the shallows away from us. Up the bank they went, breaking into the rocking trot I had been afraid I'd never see, and then we caught a last glimpse of them against the hill, between yellowing poplars.

We went home in triumph. Through a thunderstorm and a sunset, both at once, a sight most weirdly glorious.

A wild magenta light on the hills, the river in deep purple shadow, a blaze of flame color lighting the thunderheads above us, while jagged lightning, electric blue, zigzagged everywhere. It was like the Doré pictures in our *Paradise Lost*.

Especially when two fallen angels came coasting down the wind into the swamp. This was almost too much! When they settled down and transformed themselves into great blue herons, I felt greatly relieved.

Tuesday, September 6th

Of course it had to be last night, just after I had seen what mammoth creatures moose are! One came along in the middle of the night, took fright at our tent, and pounded off through the woods like a runaway locomotive. Such crashes from an Oriniack! I'm quite sure now I'd rather see than hear one.

64

I lay awake a long while, looking out at the dark, feeling that over-mastering awe of the black night and its terrors which is our inheritance from savage ancestors.

But I want the alarums as well as the excursions; I wouldn't want to miss the discords of these wild fastnesses.

We broke camp early this morning and fished on our way down the river, which was held captive in nets of white fog. I caught three bass, and we watched a mink wander along the shore, like a country gentleman out for a stroll.

We came out into the wide lake again. There was never a morning so completely flawless. Sky-blue water, wide shores backed by the dim lilac of pine ranges, great cloud foams of white and lavender piled up far behind them. Yet shore and clouds, great as they were, only a narrow strip between the pure blue above and below. When these big lakes are still — do you remember, when you were small, they filled a glass of water full for you, and then put on one more drop, so that the water stood up over the edge of the glass? These lakes seem overfull of beauty, like that, and sometimes I can hardly bear it.

September 7th

This is, I think, the most perfect camp of all. How can I say that, when they are all so different? When our three sapphire lakes were so especially glamorous? But that was a misted fairytale place. This is a clear carved design — true poetry.

It is so savagely sweet here; a pagan loveliness — Grecian paganism, untouched and pure. With all its wildness you would never be afraid.

Yesterday we meant to explore the bays on Lac la Croix. But on a small wild-rice bay there was a tantalizing portage to Lake McAree, and we found ourselves over here.

In the afternoon, I saw an Elysian island ahead of us and begged for it. There seemed no place to land, but it looked so mysteriously perfect

66

we went all around it, and found at last a secluded horseshoe to the north, where we could push in between fallen trees and water plants.

This island seemed never to have had anyone set foot on it. A most ancient and primeval place, all deep shadows and thick green moss and queer tall boulders. No wide sunny spaces, only bits of gold. Dark hollows filled with densely matted pine needles and vine tangles, doubled twisted trees leaning low over the water. There was no place to camp at all. But we felt held here, like Rat and Mole from *The Wind in the Willows;* we expected to hear the mighty Piper at any moment.

A little farther on we found a sunnier island, and another darker one, with a small and shimmering bay between. As we came into it, six mallard ducks were swimming there. They flew up as we came close, and went skimming around us and off over the trees.

As we went on, a single duck, flying up from the woods, went south and then came circling back. This was the mother duck, Lee was sure, and her children had already disappeared.

On through a narrow channel with a clean pine wood on the east shore, and around the corner we found a lily pond, peaceful and silvered; then we went past a point to a wide blue lake again. We didn't need to see any more. We came back through the inlet, and after hesitating between the clear pine wood and the sunlit island, we somehow chose the island.

When we landed, the great pine trunks were gilded with light, and ferns and mats of blueberries were enameled mosaics, gold, green-gold, and green-blue. There was a breath of scented wind, and then we heard a hermit thrush singing, the first one we have heard in our canoe country. That most haunting gold-dark song, golden with realized rapture, dark with unrealized grief — I shall never hear it again without longing for this place.

Lee made our camp above a ledge of rocks, in the midst of treetops. It was the hottest middle of the afternoon and I lay on my back in gray moss, soft and thick, in the shadow of the widest pine, and began a poem,

When the blue light comes
Through the great pine wood,
Clear and unblown
As blue light should —

while Lee chopped down trees with reckless enjoyment, and the mother duck flew wildly over the island, calling for her children.

When it was cooler and long shadows flung themselves down the hill, I cooked supper, while Lee cleaned the fish I had caught on the way down. I picked blueberries by the bush; it's quicker that way, and they make an exotic centerpiece, with the luminous berries, exquisite as flowers, and the pointed leaves now turned to crimson lacquer.

I had my most attractive place for camp cooking. A crack down the rocks for my fireplace, the flat top of the stony ledge for my table, and glimpses through interlaced boughs, over islands and golden water. Lee chopped a path down through the ash trees to the east shore, a little vista through green leaves, down to green ripples and slim reeds.

I was so enchanted with our home that I made a blueberry shortcake for supper, the first baking I've tried, using sweetened biscuit dough for the cake and the largest of my covered pots for an oven. It was a flagrant triumph.

As we ate supper we could see the blue night coming up the eastern sky. Blue night over there, and it was approaching us, step by step. I had never seen it come so unmistakably. It grew darker, and the small moon brightened. The shores and islands became black blots, and the moon began to make a faint rainbow path on the lake.

This half-moon made everything around us more solitary. I suppose because I've watched just such a moon so often at home. The island felt *farther away* than any place I've ever been.

Lee and I sat on the cliff's edge. Our duck came swimming around the island, from moonlight to dark shadow, still calling her lost children. She was so small a figure in the night, and she wasn't calling frantically now, but in a subdued way, reassuringly and tenderly.

When at last the mosquitoes drove us into our tent, there was still a view, through the netting, of black branches and a great emerald star.

Wild clouds, too, that grew wilder and heavier, till a terrific storm broke in the west. The lightning and thunder became almost continuous and the wind whooped in the trees. Lee got really worried about the tent's blowing away.

"Shall we pack everything?" he said. "Though if the tent goes it will be so tragic that all the little things might as well blow away too!"

We grew more and more hilarious as the wind blew harder and harder, and I laughed so at Lee's trying to hold on to three corners of the tent at once, dashing around like one of our chipmunks, that I could hardly hold the one corner I was responsible for.

We even made up songs about the tent, hoping it would be flattered enough to stay with us, and from that we progressed to all the old songs we'd ever known. It must have been surprising to the owls to hear

> *"Steamboat Bill, steaming down the Mississippi,*
> *Tryin' to break the record of the Robert E. Lee!"*

coming from an unsteady small tent, rocking on a rockbound shore, in the middle of a thunderstorm and the middle of the night.

September 9th

Ten days now since we've seen any human beings. It's quite a record. I haven't missed them at all.

This morning was washday. Down the path Lee had cleared, I carried my laundry to the jade-green pool shielded by lemon-scented bushes. Blackberry vines curled near. Some delicate dry grasses of pale cream

71

stood against the brilliant water. I splashed and rubbed my clothes on the stones and felt very archaic.

Spreading my array on the bushes to dry, I retreated to the pine shade. Here the moss was soft and brightly green, and I lay full length in it. So I discovered its flowers.

Flowers of the moss. I'd like to make a diminutive study of them. Shallow cups of pale green, bright scarlet tips enameled on green stems, tarnished silver discs. Coral dots, tawny seed pods high on slender threads, brown-petaled cups, gold points, rose points, gray-green trumpets. There is a deep gray moss like masses of tiny shrubs, a green velvet that covers stones as smoothly as upholstery, a pale green lichen like minute oak leaves. All these atoms are so *sturdy* in their miniature loveliness. I want to keep them.

This afternoon we came over to the ancient island. I am drifting around in the canoe, while Lee has gone ashore to sketch.

I'm in the bottom of the canoe, lying back against our coats. It's very still. Just a little lapping of the water on the stone near me — that's the only sound. Now and then I can hear Lee crashing somewhere on the island.

Such deep gloom up through the trees! Down here there are water plants whose graceful curled leaves start deep in the brown water, and reeds whose slender jointed stems sway high above the flat lily pads. Long swaths of grass lie on the liquid surface in irregular circles. Over the water a Norway pine swoops down; its lovely horizontal branches, its blue-green needles and rough twigs are reflected sharply. There are tiny warblers flying all through it, like truant piano notes. I'm so happy I can almost fly too.

We have been down to the rapids fishing. I laughed till I cried down there; any whoops the loons made were nothing to mine. As I stepped out of the canoe the rock was slippery and my foot slid into the water. Lee has been training me, ever since we started, in the proper way to enter

72

and leave a canoe, so now he said reprovingly, "No sense in that!" Then *he* stepped steadily out, on the same treacherous stone, and went, *zipp*, down on his back in the lake. I never saw such an amazed expression. "No sense in that, Lee!" I said sternly.

September 10th

The sunset yesterday was Blake's "eternity in an hour." Great bubbles of clouds, cream and soft fire and amethyst, floating over all the world, in a sky so boundless that the world was only a small, dimmer bubble itself. When I lay back against the rocks, and looked up into the intense soft blue, with great circles of pink and rose and soft lilac gleaming there, I was transformed from an earth creature into an airy one.

Feeling so light in spirit, I went canoeing. Lee remained lazily on shore, but I set out alone without a qualm. Only, when I got out into the lake and gusts of wind assailed me, I realized suddenly that it had been absolutely calm on the former occasions when I had been sole navigator. And then I had had a load to steady the canoe. Now it was empty-headed and as hard to control as most empty-headed people are. Its bow rose defiantly in the air. I couldn't manage to keep any direction. I bobbed around like a circus horse.

Lee began to shout from the shore, but his advice was mostly blown away. I felt as frantic as I do when I'm talking excitedly over the telephone and the family keeps calling additions and contradictions from the next room! In trying to follow the remnants of counsel which came to me, and to control my canoe and my laughter, I somehow got a violent cramp in my right hand.

Now I did curvet wildly! I couldn't get the bow headed toward the island; the wind spun me back every time. I was amazed at the canoe, usually so obedient to Lee's slightest gesture; it was up in arms against me. With no authority at all, I went drifting down the lake to an unknown destination.

I began to have misgivings. What *was* going to happen to me? It looked as if I might blow across the lake.

If I did that, I'd have to wait on the far shore till the wind went down. Probably I'd be there all night. I had no matches with me for a fire — not even a coat for a cover. And Lee would be frightened about me. For that matter I'd be horribly frightened about myself. In the mornings we always found footprints of things that had walked along the shores in the night. I didn't want to stay on a dark shore and meet them. But I'd never dare go back into the forest depths —

I looked despairingly back at Lee, safe on our cliff.

He was just giving me up as hopeless. Resignedly, as I watched, he sat down and began to unlace his boots.

The next thing I knew he was swimming to the mainland, and then he came dashing along the rocks, parallel to my course. But I was in the lee of the island now, and sheltered from the wind; so by peculiar paddling I managed to approach the shore. Lee waded out and boarded the craft, and I was ignominiously wafted homeward.

I began to wish I hadn't laughed so unrestrainedly at Lee in the afternoon. It had set a bad example.

"No sense in this, my dear! No sense in this! — And if it hadn't been for that spot of calm I suppose I'd be galloping for miles around all those deep bays, to keep you from going down the rapids at the end of the lake!"

But in spite of his hilarity I found myself hoping that he would *not* break his strong right arm, or even his left one. In fact I hoped fervently that nothing at all would happen to him. For it was evident that if anything did, it would take me years to get us back to Winton.

I awoke in the middle of the night to feel deeply thankful that I was safe on our island and not stranded on some solitary shore. I got up and slipped out of the tent to see what midnight was really like. Under an ink-black pine, looking out over the dim water, I felt strange and small.

The wind had died. The stillness had an inexplicable poignancy. Those immensities of land and water — they belonged to porcupines walking in the moonlight, to slender deer, and heavy shuffling bears.

I tried to picture this region in midwinter. The flawless white. Snowy hills, snowy pines with glints of hidden jade, vast levels of snowy lake. A drifted purity broken only by track patterns, from the tiny footprints of the wood mice to the great crashes of the moose. The frosted vapor coming up from the rapids, encrusting the branches with silver, drifting down the shores like the ghosts of the caribou that used to wander here. Deer standing on their hind legs to eat the cedars, a pileated woodpecker shocking the snowy silence with his scarlet and white and black. Timber wolves trotting along the ice, skirting the shores—

And at that I heard a wolf howl, far down the lake. Again the howl came, unmistakable. After the blood-curdling moose call, this seemed only pleasantly eerie, especially as it was a distant sound. Still, I went inside the tent again.

This afternoon we went over to the lily pond to read *The King's Henchman*. White water lilies lay on the black water; white birches, delicate poplars, and dark cedars were mingled on three sides. On the fourth was a gigantic hill, with straight Norway pines towering up magnificently between moss-deep rocks. Their strength was a powerful contrast to all the lacelike beauty near by.

We climbed into the branches of a pine which hung far out over the water, and dangled our feet and read Millay to our hearts' content. Then we swam in the ebony pool — so different from our usual sunny beaches — and tried picking water lilies under water.

Tomorrow we start retracing our path, so I suppose my notebook will end here. I've just noticed that I never seem to write down the last few days in any of our journeys. Probably because when my thoughts begin to turn with joy toward home, I don't want to realize the fact of departure. Probably, too, I am not as deep in the moment's adventure. Not that there is less enjoyment in these hours, but we are already changing from the present to the future tense. And then I never like to say good-by.

Lee is hurrying now to finish his sketch of the deep forest, before the light fails. It is his last chance, for we are starting out at dawn tomorrow morning.

It is time for us to go. The food pack is very light to lift. There is a look of autumn in the sunlight now, though no frosty air has touched us. The blueberry leaves have been crimson ever since we've been here, but now the stray birches are shining yellow among the dark pines down the shore.

Yet we do not need to hurry too fast on our way back, for we have five days left before we must reach Winton. We mean to take practically the same paths and portages. The leaves along the stony hills will be flaming gold and scarlet soon — we are looking forward to that.

But I don't want to leave. I'll always remember this place and long for it a little. Islands of gold and green, the wind in great branches, an owl's call in the rainy dusk, the scent of our wood smoke drifting across the moonlight. It will be like a lost kingdom.

ACKNOWLEDGMENTS

In so informal and personal a book as this, a conventional preface in the usual place might have come between the reader and the good companions who were sharing their experience with him. But now that the journey is ended, and the spell broken, we can thank those who made it possible.

First, of course, Mrs. Jaques, who graciously consented to expand into a book sketches contributed to the *American Girl* and to the *Portal*. To the discerning editors of these magazines we make grateful acknowledgment of the permission to reprint those parts of the book which appeared in their pages.

And equally Mr. Jaques, for complementing his wife's sensitivity and gaiety with his knowledge of the wilderness and with the sure vigor and beauty of his drawing. Mr. Jaques' bird habitat groups in the American Museum of Natural History are the delight of thousands. His paintings illustrate *Florida Bird Life*, *The Birds of Minnesota*, and *Oceanic Birds of South America;* he has done black and white sketches for many of the books by Dr. Frank M. Chapman. Some of the drawings in this book are adapted from illustrations for an article in *Natural History*. We thank its editors for permission to use them in this way.

The Publishers

Florence Page Jaques (1890–1972) and **Francis Lee Jaques** (1887–1969) wrote and illustrated eight books together. They met in New York City and were married in 1927; their honeymoon, a canoe trip through the Minnesota–Ontario Boundary Waters, was described in *Canoe Country*, published in 1938. They returned to experience "the same land in another guise" during the winter of 1943–44, and *Snowshoe Country* was published in 1944; it received the prestigious John Burroughs Medal as an outstanding nature book. Their other books are *The Geese Fly High* (Minnesota, 1939), *Birds across the Sky* (1942), *Canadian Spring* (1947), *As Far as the Yukon* (1951), and *There Once Was a Puffin and Other Nonsense Verses* (1957).

Lee Jaques was one of America's great nature and wildlife artists. He was a background painter for the American Museum of Natural History in New York City and also painted dioramas for the James Ford Bell Museum of Natural History at the University of Minnesota. His autobiography, *Francis Lee Jaques: Artist of the Wilderness World*, was completed by Florence and published after his death.